MW00490888

HAPPY VET HAPPY PET

CARING FOR YOUR PET'S CAREGIVER

SANDY WEAVER

Happy Vet Happy Pet

First published in 2021 by

Panoma Press Ltd
48 St Vincent Drive, St Albans, Herts, AL1 5SJ, UK
info@panomapress.com
www.panomapress.com

Book layout by Neil Coe.

978-1-784529-31-4

The right of Sandy Weaver to be identified as the author of this work has been asserted in accordance with sections 77 and 78 of the Copyright, Designs and Patents Act 1988.

A CIP catalogue record for this book is available from the British Library.

All rights reserved. No part of this book may be reproduced in any material form (including photocopying or storing in any medium by electronic means and whether or not transiently or incidentally to some other use of this publication) without the written permission of the copyright holder except in accordance with the provisions of the Copyright, Designs and Patents Act 1988. Applications for the copyright holder's written permission to reproduce any part of this publication should be addressed to the publishers.

This book is available online and in bookstores.

Copyright 2020 Sandy Weaver

Dedication

For Sandy Karn, DVM and Rebecca Kestle, DVM…
the two best friends any pet-owner could have for her
dogs, and the two best vets any pets ever had.

Foreword

My profession – a profession that I love – has a problem. It's a problem that has gone largely unrecognized by those not within its ranks. While everyone knows that medical professionals experience a great deal of stress, few realize that veterinarians hold the unique position as the professionals at highest risk for suicide related to stress, from feelings of helplessness, hopelessness and a variety of other factors.

One person who has recognized our problem and has dedicated herself to try to help is Sandy Weaver, the Program Director and a prominent speaker for the Center for Workplace Happiness. She brings tools to her clients to improve their engagement and wellness, dealing with topics such as Meditation, Happiness on the Job, and Becoming Radiantly Resilient. She is an American Veterinary Medical Association-certified workplace wellbeing expert and has penned this book as part of her outreach on behalf of our profession. One of her passions is ending suicide in our ranks. She seeks to end this scourge, as far too many veterinarians have been tragically lost already. Sandy and I connected on LinkedIn and are affiliated through her pet's veterinary hospital, BluePearl Veterinary Partners.

As friends, clients, and co-workers of veterinarians, we may be in a unique position to make a difference by being aware of triggers for their stress and ways to intervene.

Whether by refining behaviors that unwittingly add to our veterinarian's stress, or by mindfully showing appreciation, or even being in tune when listening is needed, people who interact with veterinarians may be there at the right place, at the right time, to help save a life.

Compassion fatigue has become an increasingly common term in the veterinary profession. This exhaustion comes from prolonged exposure to other people's trauma. When you come into your veterinarian's office or emergency clinic with a crisis, it is often the first and only scary and traumatic time you have shared with your pet and your veterinarian. For your veterinarian, a crisis like that happens day after day, week after week, and year after year. And veterinarians – the good ones, anyway – have deep empathy and compassion for each and every pet under their care. But this compassion is not given without a cost. This continuous outpouring of compassion drains the mental fuel needed for your veterinarian to recharge, refresh, and deal with life outside his or her practice. Rather than giving less than the full attention you and your pet need, most veterinarians are at risk of short-changing the other aspects of their lives. Sometimes the reserves just run out.

Keep in mind that most veterinarians see their career as a calling. They approach every day with passion. They thrive on helping and healing your pet. They also have extensive experience at helping you let go at the end of your pet's life. My wife, a physician, notes that pets and their owners are given dignity in death, while humans face prolonged suffering, pointless and costly treatments, with the same inevitable end. In human medicine, they do the heroic measures because they can. Medicare pays tremendously for end of life care, but physicians and families alike question whether treatment prolongs life or prolongs suffering. However, with pet care, clients expect advanced medical treatments for their beloved family pets but face the realities of the high costs of these advanced treatments. Sadly this often leaves the client weighing the options between going into debt to pay for care or resorting to euthanasia. Imagine how disappointing your life would be – you've nailed a tricky diagnosis and recommended a thoughtful treatment plan which you can skillfully perform, only to have the plan refused due to the cost, and the visit culminates in euthanasia.

Veterinarians spend many years in training with 8 years of college/veterinary school and 2-6 years for specialty training, with expertise in the care of many species, and they incur a tremendous amount of debt obtaining their education. They do not have a choice but to charge for their knowledge and services to pay for their educational investment, meet payroll and rent, and lead a balanced life.

Compared with human doctors, veterinarians' salaries are not commensurate with the years of education invested. For them, there is nothing more heartbreaking than to achieve a diagnosis and have the skill set to treat a pet through surgery and medicine only to know that all that work and planning comes to nothing unless the client can afford the care and follow your recommendations. Otherwise, rather than healing that beautiful animal, you are asked to provide more affordable but less effective treatments or provide euthanasia. That hurts on a whole different level – and it happens all the time. They cannot choose to provide free care and stay in business.

Knowing that their treatment can make a difference but won't have the opportunity to provide it causes career dissatisfaction, burnout, depression, and all too often, pain that just won't go away.

I have been a veterinarian, business owner, active member in veterinary associations, and educator for more than 40 years. I have witnessed the veterinary profession grow leaps and bounds from single one-veterinarian private practices to corporate-owned practice groups. I have been the primary caretaker to many wonderful pets, and ultimately the decision-maker (and the one to push the medication) to end the lives of my family members' pets. I began dreading that eventuality from the day I graduated from veterinary college. Can you imagine the stress that brings to friendships and family life?

The times of a veterinarian providing all the services in their own hospital have evolved with the advent of specialty hospitals. We now have the ability to refer complex cases to board-certified veterinarians at academic institutions and regional specialty practices across our nation. With increasing choice and better evidence-based care, knowledgeable clients' demands will continue to escalate with higher expectations for advanced knowledge and treatment. The trends towards big business in veterinary medicine will likely push out many private practices, but not all corporate models of care will be based on best practices or "best care and feeding" of their employed veterinarians. As a result, the care for our clients' beloved family pets may also suffer, along with the continued stressors for the veterinarians who know best care but are not rewarded by practicing it.

Our clients often present with their pets and cannot describe their concerns well, and the pets may not exhibit symptoms of their illness. Veterinarians are gifted with the ability to recognize signs and diagnose the illness in their non-verbal patients, but at the same time often can't recognize the signs of stress-causing illness in our veterinary colleagues who may be contemplating suicide. The signs may be subtle, but you are ahead of the game if you know what you are looking for. Veterinarians are not likely to attempt suicide. They complete suicide. They have often spent decades comforting clients with well-honed platitudes that euthanasia is a gift to take away pain and needless suffering. They know that it works.

I lost one of my veterinary partners of 20 years to suicide. He was a brilliant veterinarian, educator, and business partner. He was well-respected by his colleagues, loved by family, friends, and co-workers, and was well-off financially. He had a great bedside manner and was very observant of the smallest changes in his patients, or his co-workers. By all respects, he seemed to have a perfect life. He often said his hobby was his career. After a business conflict, he decided to retire. With this, he seemed to lose his drive and identity. Just the week before he completed suicide, he declined my invitation to join me for a musical venue that he normally would have enjoyed. At the time, I didn't think anything of it. That is until I learned more about the signs of impending suicide. I was not alone. Not even the people who knew him well recognized the signs. We did not have an opportunity to try to prevent the loss of such a great colleague.

I hope this book will give you insights into the complicated stressors veterinarians manage on a daily basis. For most clients, their veterinarian is a part of the family. Always, even late at night or on weekends, they are there to guide you or to save or help your beloved pet. Sometimes the connection is the friendship of the client, and other times the friendship is with their pet. The time of your need may coincide with an unimaginable need of theirs. With your veterinarian, as with all those whom you hold dear, be in tune and be willing to listen, to ask, to care. Read this book! Let's not lose another veterinarian.

The veterinarian you save may be your own!

Dr. Gary L. Modrcin DVM, DAVDC

Board Certified in Veterinary Dentistry

Co-founder BluePearl Veterinary Partners

Founder College Boulevard Animal Hospital

Past President of the Kansas Veterinary Medical Association

Past President of Kansas City Veterinary Medical Association

Past Chairman of Credentials Committee of the American Veterinary Dental College

Foreword dedicated to the memory of Jeff S. Dennis DVM, DACVIM

Contents

Contents

Introduction

You're about to read a book that will change your relationship with your veterinarian and their team. Forever. You need to be OK with that before you keep reading.

> The information in this book is not just life-changing; it's lifesaving.

Still here? Great! Because what happens once you've learned a few hard truths and three really easy ones will change your life and may save someone else's.

Yes, you read that right – the information in this book is not just life-changing; it's lifesaving. Trust me on that for right now – by the time you've read the first four chapters, you'll know beyond a shadow of a doubt the truth of that "lifesaving" part. Don't stop after the first four chapters though – the next two will guide you in how to use that information like a super-power, for the good of your pets, your vet, their team and even pets, vets and veterinary teams you'll never meet.

The reason I've written this book is because, like Not One More Vet, Inc. https://www.nomv.org/ I'm on a mission to save lives. When the CDC report on veterinary suicide came out in January of 2019, I wasn't surprised at the fact that veterinary suicide is a problem. That's been anecdotally understood for years, and I even knew a veterinarian who completed suicide. I was appalled at the size and scope of the problem and that the bulk of veterinary suicides are doctors and technicians working in small animal practices. With over 260,000,000 pets in the US https://www.americanpetproducts.org/press_industrytrends.asp those small animal practices are vital to the health and wellbeing of our furry, feathered, and finned friends and are the very doctors and technicians most at risk of suffering from suicidal desperation.

> There's a tendency to think of veterinarians as smart people who get to play with puppies and kittens all day. What could vets possibly be stressed about?

When I share with pet-owners the issue of suicide in the veterinary community, the most common reaction is an open-mouthed gasp and the word, "why?"

There's a tendency to think of veterinarians as smart people who get to play with puppies and kittens all day. They spend their days surrounded by sweet animals with loving owners and a competent staff who does the dirty work. What could vets possibly be stressed about?

Here's the reality – the pets are usually stressed to be in a vet hospital, and most aren't on their best behavior. The owners often feel like the professional fees are too high, the recommended treatment isn't necessary, and according to what they read on the internet, the vet has the wrong diagnosis. And the staff is human – sometimes cranky, sometimes hormonal, and sometimes they don't show up for work, leaving the hospital short-staffed and stressed-out.

And we pet-owners and pet-lovers who think we're doing things right often add to the veterinarian's stress without meaning to, knowing it or even thinking about it. I've done it, and you probably have too. No judgment – just a desire to ease the stress of the people we count on to care for our pets.

So, now that you have full disclosure on what reading this book will do to you and for you, let's just dive right in, shall we? Knowing how to care for your pet's caregiver might just save their life!

CHAPTER 1

A Day in the Life of a Veterinarian

In this chapter, let me introduce you to Dr. Jan Smith. She is a compilation of many veterinarians I interviewed for this book. Pieces of her life are shared by most or all of those vets, and some of the finer details came from the lives of just a handful of them. I "created" Dr. Smith from the wisdom, experiences, sacrifices, and tears I heard in those interviews.

Dr. Smith is a veterinarian. She's in her early 40's and is the owner of a small, one-doctor vet practice. She's married with two children, one in elementary school and one in middle school. Her husband is the sales manager at a luxury car dealership near their home.

While together they earn a good living, the topic of finances causes stress in the marriage – neither has a paycheck that is a regular, dependable amount, and the earning power of each is dependent in part on the strength of the economy, as well as what people post about them on social media. One of their monthly payments is repayment of student loans. Even though she's been in practice for over a decade, the balance due is still substantial. The Smiths thought they'd have the loans paid off before buying a practice, but it didn't work out that way.

Because Dr. Smith's practice is a small business, there is that added financial stress – a staff to pay, payroll taxes, medical insurance for her team and her family, a hospital note to pay, equipment to pay for, outside lab fees to pay, marketing expenses to pay, government regulations to remain conversant on and compliant with, and an accountant to oversee all of it – for a fee, of course. It would ease a lot of work stress for Dr. Smith if she could hire a hospital manager. She and her husband don't see a way to add that salary to the rest of their monthly payments, at least not at this point.

Family time is precious – Dr. Smith works five and a half days a week because she's the only doctor in her practice. Her husband's responsibilities also keep him busy, often working weeknights and always working Saturdays. The children are on sports teams and take music lessons, and it's usually the parents of their friends who take them to and from those activities.

Dr. Smith loves her staff. Most of them have been employed in that hospital since she first came to the practice nearly a decade ago. She was the associate vet then – the former owner of the practice brought her on in the hopes that he could sell her the practice and retire. She worked as an associate for four years, helping the practice grow a little bit, and purchased it when the owner decided to call it quits. The staff stayed on, which was both a good and not-so-good thing. One of the techs occasionally behaves as if she knows more than Dr. Smith does, and the receptionist has been known to be a bit passive-aggressive. For the most part, the team works well together, so Dr. Smith does her best to ignore the misbehavior.

Buying the hospital was a stretch, financially, and also the culmination of a long-held dream. Even though Dr. Smith was still paying off student loans from her years in college and vet school, she jumped at the chance to be the owner of the practice so she could stand in the grown-up career shoes she'd dreamed of since she was 12.

What she didn't bargain for was the change in her responsibilities – she went from focusing solely on caring for clients' pets as an associate veterinarian to focusing mainly on running the hospital. Now, instead of walking through the front door of the hospital each morning and finding out what her appointment schedule held for her, she's often greeted with something like, "the lab didn't pick up the specimens again last night" or "Ryan isn't coming in to do the kennels today so who's going to take care of that?" or even "we're out of toilet paper – did you remember to stop and get some?"

As she heads to her paper-strewn desk, Dr. Smith feels some tension in the air. Celia, the receptionist, seems grumpy as she talks to a client on one line, with another line on hold. She makes a mental note to ask if everything is OK once Celia's off the phone.

She checks her voice mails and emails, making notes of charts to pull and review before she can return the messages. She thumbs through the stack of papers and charts Celia put on the desk this morning, looking at lab results and making a note to call those owners too.

As she looks at her appointment schedule she sees:

1. Check-in: dog for spay

2. Check-in: dog for tumor removal

3. Scheduled – three dogs and a cat that the owners will drop off in the morning. Dogs need annual vax and nail trim, cat isn't eating

4. An elderly, beloved dog who's been declining lately

5. A canine annual visit

6. A puppy wellness check with microchip, vaccines, and deworming

7. A difficult cat with a tendency for bladder crystals

8. A delightful cat with a difficult owner who imagines ailments and argues about fees

9. A suture removal on a sweet old dog
    – Break for lunch, surgeries and seeing the pets that were dropped off

10. A newly-adopted dog with a skin issue

11. Euthanasia

12. Initial appointment – new client with a new kitten

13. (open)

14. Dog who might have eaten a sock

15. Recheck and bloodwork – dog with Cushing's disease

16. Dog throwing up for two days

17. A canine annual visit – two dogs

Dr. Smith sighed. She knew the day was coming that the Champions' dog was going to come in for euthanasia, and she had dreaded it. This is the first pet she treated when she started working at this hospital. She and the owners had developed a strong relationship throughout their Golden Retriever's life, and she knew how much losing him would hurt them. And her, too, she realized.

The rest of the day looked pretty normal – she might be home in time to make dinner for her children, depending on how the afternoon went. The three biggest wild cards were the potential sock-eater, the vomiting dog, and the kitty dropped off because it wasn't eating. From experience, she knew those three could take more than their 20 minutes on the schedule.

Before starting to return calls, Dr. Smith went to the front desk to check on Celia, see if her surgery animals were ready for their pre-surgery physical and whether the dogs and cat listed as drop-offs were in the hospital yet.

Celia was still grumpy, irritated by a client who wanted advice but not an appointment and irritated at a tech who wasn't moving fast enough in Celia's estimation. Basically, it seemed like Celia was irritated at the world, so Dr. Smith made a mental note to steer clear of her if possible, at least until lunchtime. Secretly she hoped the bad mood would just go away, though from experience, she knew that wasn't likely. Dr. Smith made yet another mental note to take Celia aside one day soon to talk about her attitude and how it affected the clients and staff. She dreaded that conversation as she headed for the treatment area to see if her surgeries were there yet.

Her lead tech, Amanda, was triaging the tumor removal dog. Amanda had been with the hospital for nearly 20 years and was technically very good. Dr. Smith remembered her early days at this hospital when it often felt like Amanda resented her presence. She behaved almost like a schoolgirl with a crush on the most popular boy in high school, only in this case that "boy" was the doctor who owned the hospital. Since he'd retired, Amanda's attitude had mellowed, though Dr. Smith occasionally heard her talking to clients as though she, not Dr. Smith, was the one making the medical decisions. Today, Amanda seemed in good spirits as she efficiently took vitals and charted them. Dr. Smith checked the cages – Tumor Removal Dog was there, Spay Dog was there, Anorexic Cat was there – the three dogs scheduled to be dropped off for annuals weren't there yet.

With forty-five minutes before her first appointment, Dr. Smith weighed her options – return calls and emails or get started on the anorexic cat. Before she could make a decision, she heard a loud crash and the sound of water flowing from down the hall and dashed out to see what happened.

A sink. On the floor of the hospital's only bathroom. Water spewing everywhere from the pipes sticking out of the wall. Celia in tears, looking guilty and pale.

Instinct kicking in, Dr. Smith ran to the main water shutoff valve, turning it tightly and completely off. The impromptu water fountain stopped, as did all water everywhere in the hospital. Great. No water for who knows how long, plus the expense of a plumber on an emergency call.

Perfect start to a perfect day. Great.

Dr. Smith tasked Celia with calling the plumber while she and Amanda cleaned up the mess in the bathroom. The sink was a goner – it was in three pieces. The drywall behind it would have to be replaced – it was a big, ragged hole that displayed three of the wall studs and two pipes bent at odd angles. Dr. Smith tried to imagine the events leading up to the crash and then decided to focus on something – anything – else. She peeked at Celia, on the phone with the plumber, and decided to try to get to the bottom of what happened later, when everyone's emotions had calmed a bit.

Once the mess was cleaned up and Dr. Smith knew the plumber was on his way, she and Amanda headed back to the treatment room to start on Anorexic Cat. The drop-off Annual Vax dogs still weren't in the hospital. They had 15 minutes until the first appointment of the day to start trying to unravel the mystery of the not-eating cat and decide whether or not they should proceed with plans for the two surgeries or send those two dogs home and reschedule them. Running water isn't optional in a veterinary hospital, especially with full kennels downstairs and surgeries and appointments upstairs.

Dr. Smith took a deep breath, closed her eyes, and weighed her options. She heard the bell on the front door announcing the arrival of her first appointment. She added to her "Mental Notes Pertaining to Celia" list and headed for the reception area.

Nodding to her first clients with their elderly dog, she leaned down to Celia to find out the plumber's schedule. Two hours before he'd be there sealed her decision – she instructed Celia to call the owners of the surgery dogs to come and pick them up and reschedule their appointments. Next on Celia's to-do list: make a sign for the front door of the hospital and the door to the bathroom, informing clients of the lack of bathroom facilities. Third, locate hand sanitizer for the lobby, the treatment area, the lab, and the exam room. If there weren't four bottles of sanitizer in the hospital, Celia was to go buy them at the convenience store on the corner. Then she was to call the owners of the three drop-off dogs and reschedule them – they could not be seen today. Call the groomer to let her know she'd need to reschedule her appointments for today and might need to reschedule tomorrow's, too. Finally, no more veterinary appointments were to be taken for the day and none for the next, either, since there was no way to know when the water situation would be resolved.

Dr. Smith ran a few quick numbers in her head and knew the cost of the sink catastrophe would be far more than just the plumber's bill. The lost surgeries, treatment visits, grooms, and client goodwill would take a big chunk out of this week's net. It could be the difference between being in the black this week or deep in the red. As part of her brain was performing this analysis, another part wondered how she'd gotten so far away from what she truly wanted to do – practice veterinary medicine and care for animals and the people who loved them.

Finally, ready to see her first client, Dr. Smith invited them back to the treatment room as she tried desperately to switch from "hospital owner with a crisis" mode to "veterinarian with a patient" mode.

The day progressed quickly as Dr. Smith focused on her patients and clients. The first client was the kind of visit she thought it would be – concerned owners who needed to know how to decide on euthanasia for their dear old, failing friend. As she counseled the dog's owners, she thought of the Champions, due to come in after lunch to put down their old dog. She snapped her brain out of that line of thought and ploughed through her morning appointments – canine annual, puppy wellness visit with vaccines, a cat-wrestling kitty urinalysis and claw-avoidance session, an annual visit with a purring kitty, suture removal from a surgery ten days ago – healing well, thankfully! – and only one difficult client to deal with all morning. She and Amanda worked like a well-oiled machine, even laughing a time or two when, from force of habit, they tried to wash their hands under dry faucets.

Somewhere between the difficult kitty and the purring kitty, the plumber showed up. With no surgeries to do, the three drop-off dogs rescheduled to the following week, and an anorexic cat still needing to be seen, Dr. Smith poked her head into the bathroom, introducing herself to the plumber. He started talking money when all Dr. Smith wanted to know was how long the job would take. Unsatisfied and apparently not likely to get a direct answer, she headed for the treatment room to work on the cat. On the way, she asked Celia to try to find out from the plumber when the hospital might have running water again.

The anorexic cat was a puzzle — she and Amanda bounced theories off of each other, analyzed the in-house bloodwork and urinalysis, and were drawing a blank. His physical exam was normal – the only chart note was that the cat needed a dental soon. The test results were fairly normal – a crystal or two in the urine and white cells slightly elevated – and yet the owner reported that the cat wasn't eating his normal food and hadn't been for a couple of days. Opening a can of prescription cat food, they watched as the kitty sniffed, snubbed, sniffed, and then dove in. He ate two tablespoons of canned ID and licked the spoon clean, looking for more. Amanda put the kitty back in his cage with a quarter of a cup of the canned food and a bowl of water while Dr. Smith pored through the unremarkable test results one more time before calling the owner. Watchful waiting, a diet of canned ID and a recheck in a week — sooner if she thought the cat's condition warranted it – and the cat could be picked up any time in the afternoon.

Lunch was a sandwich and a bottle of water at her desk while she returned the calls and emails from the morning. She had a rhythm – look at the client's name, the patient's name, then the message about what was going on, then the patient's chart before calling or emailing. That part of the job took about 45 minutes today, though some days it took longer and some days less. She walked the charts back to Celia for re-filing and asked what the plumber had said about turning the water back on.

Not today. Maybe tomorrow afternoon. He had someone who could do the drywall repair coming this afternoon, and once the drywall was up and mudded, it would be late tomorrow morning at the earliest before he could re-hang the sink. He had repaired the pipes, readying them to be tied back into the new sink. Once the sink was hung, it was just a matter of making the connections, and he could turn the water back on.

Dr. Smith was frustrated. Since the pipes were repaired, why wasn't he offering to cap them off so they could have water back on right now? She and her husband had done that during a kitchen remodel, and it worked fine. Dr. Smith voiced that question, and the plumber looked irritated. He turned on his heel and headed for his truck. Five minutes later he came back with a soldering iron, solder, copper caps, and a level of irritation that matched Celia's earlier in the day.

Could no one do their jobs competently? Why, thought Dr. Smith, did she have to be the one to suggest solutions? And what's with the attitude? Wasn't she the customer? Why didn't he come up with the solution, and now why was he behaving like a baby because he had to do it her way – the way that would allow her to run her hospital so she could pay his bill?

She realized she needed to take a break from this drama, so she headed back to her office. Time to look at this afternoon's patients and their charts so she could be ready to care for them, not spar with someone she'd probably never see again after tomorrow. He was going on her "do not call again" list. On the way to her office, she asked Celia to call the groomer to let her know that the water would be back on soon so she could arrange her clients accordingly. She reminded Celia to take down the sign on the front door when the plumber turned the water back on but to leave the one on the bathroom door in place until the next day. Until the sink was functional, the toilet was off-limits to clients.

The afternoon flew by and was a roller-coaster of emotions. She could barely concentrate on the client with the skin-issue dog because she knew the Champions and their Golden were on the way. She was her best professional self while discussing the euthanasia with them, letting them know that they had made the kindest, most loving decision for their friend, letting them know how the sequence of drugs would act once administered through his vein, what would probably happen – he'd relax, drift off, and his heart would stop – as well as what could happen – an agonal breath, causing a spasm that made it seem as though he was still conscious when in fact he wasn't. When they were ready, she administered the drugs through tear-filled eyes. She left them with her condolences and his body and went to her office and cried.

Two of the afternoon appointments were no-show, no-call. The rest were routine – the potential sock-eater showed nothing on x-ray, the Cushing's dog was well-controlled, the vomiting dog was put on electrolytes, a 24-hour fast, and then a bland diet – recheck in a week, or sooner if the vomiting continued. The last appointment of the day – the canine annuals for two dogs – was one of the no-shows. This had not been a good day financially in her hospital. Not by a long shot.

Dr. Smith sat at her desk, arranging the piles of paper into neat stacks that might make sense tomorrow morning. Sitting there, she realized her shoulders were tense, and her jaw was clenched. She wondered how long that had been going on as she tried to relax her shoulders down to where they were supposed to be.

Celia. What was she going to say to Celia? That question had been nagging at her all day. How could she have a conversation about her irritability with clients and staff and, at the same time, find a reasonable way to ask how the sink managed to fling itself on the floor? It felt like that needed to be two conversations, neither of which Dr. Smith felt up to having today. And yet, the longer she waited, the harder the conversation would be. For the hundredth time, at least, Dr. Smith found herself fantasizing about being able to hire a hospital manager. Maybe she'd float the idea again tonight with her husband, once he finally got home from the dealership. And only if he was in a good mood.

Dr. Smith gathered up her things and headed to the front door. Celia was on the phone, and Dr. Smith was secretly relieved – no conversations tonight. She thought maybe she'd bring enough lunch for both of them tomorrow and invite Celia to eat and chat. That might work, as long as tomorrow didn't explode like today did.

On the way home, Dr. Smith went through the drive-through for dinner. She hated herself for doing this – it felt like she was a failure as a mother, feeding her children this way – and yet she didn't know what was in the kitchen that could be whipped up with minimal effort, and she was drained. Done. Not cooking. Maybe not even eating – she'd get plenty for the four of them and let the kids eat what they wanted. Then she'd see if her husband was hungry when he got home – if so, she'd warm up the other two meals for them and eat a few bites. The bottle of wine in the refrigerator was calling her name – while her kids ate, she'd catch up with them while trying to unwind from her day.

After the kids were fed, helped with homework, and tucked into their bedrooms, if not their actual beds, Dr. Smith plopped on the couch, wine glass in hand. Scrolling through her phone as she waited for her husband to come home, she saw an email from the owner of the anorexic cat, asking how much food to give him. It came through the hospital email account, not her personal one, and at this time of night, it was too late to usefully answer that question. She felt like she'd failed that client, at least a little bit, and made a mental note to call her in the morning before she started seeing clients.

Her husband came in, excited about making his monthly quota just ten days into the month. Dr. Smith was happy that one of them had a good day – she let him tell her all about the turn-around a difficult saleswoman had made while they ate fast-food and drank the rest of the wine, then together cleaned up the kitchen, readied the coffee pot for the next morning and then both plopped on the couch.

Somehow the hospital manager topic didn't get brought up. Dr. Smith thought about bringing it up and knew what her husband would say – even though he'd had a great day, their budget was still tight and unlikely to improve much until they could get the student loans paid off or until there were enough clients in the hospital to pay for an associate vet.

Both of those eventualities felt eons away, especially after the day she'd had. And the day she was dreading already — tomorrow she had to make herself have a difficult conversation with Celia. Over lunch. Which she hadn't made yet, for her or her kids.

She thought about other veterinarians and wondered if they struggled with days like this. She wondered if they ever felt like a bad parent, or like they'd let a client down, or like they'd never be able to make enough money to dig themselves out of debt so they'd finally be able to add to their hospital staff so they could grow. She wondered how they coped with difficult clients and difficult staff members and difficult contractors. She wondered whether she'd sleep tonight or if it would be another night of waking up at 3 a.m., mind racing over everything she did wrong the day before and might do wrong that day.

She wondered how she could have been so wrong about what being a veterinarian really meant.

CHAPTER 2

Just Who Are Veterinarians, Anyway?

Did you know that veterinarians take an oath when becoming a vet? Here's what they promise themselves, their peers, their clients, and their patients:

"Being admitted to the profession of veterinary medicine, I solemnly swear to use my scientific knowledge and skills for the benefit of society through the protection of animal health, the relief of animal suffering, the conservation of livestock resources, the promotion of public health, and the advancement of medical knowledge. I will practice my profession conscientiously, with dignity, and in keeping with the principles of veterinary medical ethics. I accept as a lifelong obligation the continual improvement of my professional knowledge and competence."

That's a big promise and is a promise veterinarians strive to keep on a daily basis. It's the bedrock of their service to their clients (human), patients (animals), and society at large. Do you stay current on the latest research on how best to do your job? Veterinarians not only promise to do it; they do it, on top of putting in 60 or more hours per week caring for their patients.

I'm guessing you're a pet-owner and have a relationship – maybe a very casual one, maybe a grand friendship, maybe something in between – with a veterinarian. When you think of your vet, what words come to mind? For a lot of people, words like these are top-of-mind:

- Compassionate
- Competent
- Smart
- Caring
- Friendly

You might be surprised to learn that the words veterinarians often use to describe themselves – their self-talk – sound more like this:

- Dumb
- Incompetent

- Imposter
- Unpopular
- Exhausted – physically and mentally

Ouch!

In truth, most human beings talk to themselves about themselves in a very negative fashion. Because of the nature of their job, and of the personality characteristics many (not all!) vets share, their negative self-talk can be very persistent and often dominates their inner life – to their detriment.

You probably innately understand that if a child is constantly told they are bad, the child will most likely feel badly about themselves and grow into a person who believes they add little value to the world around them. It is the rare human being who can take that constant barrage of negativity and make a positive life out of it. Children raised with predominantly negative messaging from their caregivers often become adults who feel a sense of hopelessness about life.

It's the same inside an adult's head – when they constantly tell themselves how dumb/incompetent/ fraudulent/unpopular/stressed they are, how do you suppose they're going to feel? And all those negative feelings just add to the day-to-day stresses of being a veterinarian, which adds to the exhaustion and, sadly, to eventual feelings of hopelessness.

It's important to understand the type of person
drawn to the veterinary profession in order to
understand why they struggle as veterinarians.

You might already know that it's tougher to get into veterinary school than it is to get into medical school. Generally, that's because there are more medical schools than veterinary schools. It's also because there are a lot of people who love animals and want to help them and choose veterinary medicine as the avenue to do so.

It's important to understand the type of person drawn to the veterinary profession in order to understand why they struggle, often on a daily basis, as veterinarians. That's what you'll discover in this chapter. First, a few numbers. If data is not your thing, skip down past the chart.

According to American Veterinary Medical Association statistics, 113,394 veterinarians were in practice in the US in 2018, https://www.avma.org/resources-tools/reports-statistics/market-research-statistics-us-veterinarians-2018

Of those, around 38% were male, almost 62% were female, and a tiny fraction didn't report a gender identity. When talking about veterinarians who are in private practice, there were 73,373 vets in 2018. Breaking the data down even further, most of the male veterinarians were concentrated in food-animal practices, and most of the female veterinarians were in companion-animal practices. Almost 67% of the 73,373 vets in private practice were in companion-animal only practices, and 64% of those veterinarians were women. If it helps to see the data in a chart, here you go:

Private Clinical Practice	Total as of 12/31/18	Percent of Total	Male %	Female %
Food animal exclusive	1,286	1.8%	77.1%	22.9%
Food animal predominant	3,105	8.7%	74.3%	25.7%
Mixed animal	4,182	5.7%	56.0%	44.0%
Companion animal predominant	6,372	8.7%	49.0%	51.0%
Companion animal exclusive	48,898	66.6%	35.9%	64.0%
Equine	4,125	5.6%	45.8%	54.2%
Other	309	0.4%	35.3%	64.7%
Species Unspecified	5,096	6.9%	21.8%	78.1%
Total Private Practice	73,373	100%	40.1%	59.9%

Is your vet a man or a woman? Looking at the companion animal categories, if your animal is a dog, cat, or other house pet, it's a good guess that your vet is female. And the gender divide is getting more pronounced every year, as more than 80% of most veterinary schools' graduates are women. All but one of the vets who have looked after my dogs through the years have been female. I jettisoned the male veterinarian fairly quickly, though his gender had nothing to do with why I fired him. That's a story for another chapter.

Most veterinarians currently in practice say they decided to enter the profession some time in their early teens. Even a tiny bit of research about what it took to get into vet school would have shown them that competition was very stiff. That means that the veterinarians currently in practice drove themselves at a very young age into straight-A-student status, did their best to excel on standardized tests, probably worked and/or volunteered at veterinary hospitals and animal shelters after school and in the summer, and were focused on the "get into vet school" goal all through their teens.

What personality type is most likely to behave that way? Here is a "broad brush" and reasonably accurate personality profile for veterinary school graduates:

- Introverted/isolated
- Perfectionist/self-critical of even the smallest perceived imperfection
- Driven/focused
- Have difficulty asking for help – feel like they should be able to handle everything
- Not a great communicator, especially where feelings are concerned

When I think of the veterinarians who have cared for my dogs, these qualities were there in each of them, to some degree. Think about your current veterinarian – do any of these qualities show up in them that you can see?

These personality traits are not innately negative or positive – they're just pieces of personality that define and often drive a person's actions. For veterinarians, it's good to be a bit of a perfectionist and to be focused. Do you want to entrust your pet's surgery to someone who is haphazard and easily distracted? Yeah – me neither!

The personality pieces that make up a great veterinarian can be the very same ones that can make them feel boxed into a corner they can't find a way out of. It's important for veterinary clients to understand our vets at a deeper level, so we don't inadvertently add to their stress.

Let's talk about introversion vs. extroversion. First, here are the generally accepted characteristics of introverts and extroverts:

https://positivepsychology.com/introversion-extroversion-spectrum/

Introvert	Extrovert
Recharge by spending time alone	Recharge by socializing
Reflect before making decisions	Make decisions quickly
Listen more	Speak more
Enjoy one-on-one conversations	Outgoing
Introspective	Easily distracted
Self-aware	Action-oriented
Think before acting	Gregarious and expressive
Learn through observation	Excellent communicator
More sociable with people they know	Enjoys being the center of attention

When it comes to being introverted or extroverted, people aren't one or the other – behavioral scientists describe a range from extremely introverted to extremely extroverted, and everyone falls somewhere between the two extremes. Most of the time, a person's level of introversion vs. extroversion will vary depending on their mood, current situation, level of comfort with the people around them, etc. In other words, while a person may tend toward introversion, their behavior in some situations could be more toward the extroverted end of the spectrum.

Here's an example: I tend to be on the introverted end of the scale. It takes a while for me to warm up to new situations and new people, and I'd rather meet new people one-on-one instead of in a networking situation or party. Those rooms full of people feel chaotic, and I must make myself attend them. The exception is when I'm the speaker at an event – then I love being in a room full of people. What's the difference? The first situation feels unpredictable, unfamiliar, and out of control. In the second, I've rehearsed and delivered enough presentations that I feel in control of myself in the situation. There have been times on the stage where things didn't go exactly as planned, yet because of past experiences, the right words just flowed out of my mouth at the right time. People who meet me as a speaker are often very surprised to discover that I'm on the introverted end of the spectrum, as that wasn't their initial experience of me.

It's not "better" to be extroverted or introverted. Both ends of the introversion/extroversion spectrum have equal value, and there are advantages and disadvantages to each. It's good to understand your own comfort level and good to understand and have compassion for the comfort level of others.

Because most veterinarians are on the introverted end of the spectrum, they prefer to spend time alone or in small groups. They are good listeners, though not always great communicators. They're at their most outgoing when with people they know, meaning the longer you've been their client, the more comfortable they'll feel around you. They are good at making decisions and make them after doing research that supports those decisions. They learn easily by seeing others learn, which also makes them good teachers. They enjoy research, puzzles, and analytical pursuits.

Sounds like the makings of a good doctor, right? Veterinary hospitals are small businesses, with one-doctor practices usually having between 5 and 20 employees. That means the doctor is in a small cocoon of well-known people on a daily basis. This is their comfort zone and can also be a potential problem. Actually, several potential problems – we'll cover those in the next chapter.

Since they're working mostly with non-veterinarians, when something goes wrong with a patient or with the staff, it's easy for them to feel like they're the only person in the world with that problem. Introverts aren't usually found mixing and mingling at networking events, so veterinarians may not have a trusted advisor or network of other vets to share with, learn from, and grow with. Since they're not always the best at talking about their own feelings or perceived shortcomings, they may not ask for advice when a problem begins to feel unmanageable. This self-isolating behavior can be a step on the slippery slope to suicide.

From 2.1 to 3.5 TIMES as likely to die by suicide as the general population. That's a lot of pain, a lot of stress and a lot of loss.

According to the Merck Animal Health Veterinary Wellbeing Study released in 2018, veterinarians are more stressed than the general population, less likely to seek professional help to manage the stress, and less likely to report that they have a healthy work/life balance.

According to the CDC study on veterinary suicide, released late in 2018 and published in the Journal of the American Veterinary Medical Association in January of 2019, female veterinarians were 3.5 times as likely, and male veterinarians were 2.1 times as likely, to die from suicide as the general population. Seventy-five percent of the veterinarians who died by suicide worked in a small animal practice: https://www.cdc.gov/media/releases/2018/p1220-veterinarians-suicide.html

From 2.1 to 3.5 TIMES as likely to die by suicide as the general population. That's a lot of pain, a lot of stress, and a lot of loss.

What it is not is a mental health crisis. Veterinarians and their teams are not suffering mental health issues at a rate higher than the general population. They are feeling more stressed than the general population.

To understand why the people who care for our beloved pets are so at risk for suicidal thoughts, suicidal desperation, and suicidal behavior, it helps to understand the stresses they're operating under and which ones are within our control to ease. Come with me to Chapter 3, where we will dive deeply into the life of a veterinarian.

CHAPTER 3

Got Stress? Your Vet Sure Does!

Let's review the list of personality traits that generally define veterinarians:

- Introverted/isolated

- Perfectionist/self-critical of even the smallest perceived imperfection

- Driven/focused

- Have difficulty asking for help – feel like they should be able to handle everything

- Not a great communicator, especially where feelings are concerned

This list is a compilation of personality profile results from veterinary students surveyed in their final year of vet school. The results reflect responses from over a thousand students, which represents about a third of students who graduate from vet schools each year in the US.

> The science load is heavy, the lab sessions are long, and the shift from "routine" to "emergency" happens often.

Think about the life of a college student going to veterinary school: they have already completed an undergraduate degree, so are into their 5th through 8th year of university studies. The science load is heavy, the lab sessions are long, the clinic hours are long, and the shift from "routine" to "emergency" happens often. Most are in school only because they were able to get student loans and must remain very focused on their studies in order to keep up their GPA so they can continue to receive financial aid.

They know that even one small failure could mean the end of their ability to fulfill their dream – to become a veterinarian.

Rushing a fraternity or sorority usually isn't a priority. Neither is getting a date for the weekend, scoring tickets to the game, or just shooting the breeze over coffee with friends.

They are focused. They are driven. They are perfectionists who are hard on themselves. They are veterinary students. The stress they practice now is the stress they will carry with them into their veterinary practice.

Let's analyze their stresses, one by one.

Money

In every research study I've seen, money is listed as the #1 stressor for veterinarians. Even if they've been in practice many years – even if they've managed to pay off their student loans – money is still a stressful topic.

In 1999, KPMG reported the findings of a study of the veterinary field: https://www.avma.org/sites/default/files/resources/161-183.pdf

Referred to as the Megastudy, it's still being used as a reference to the health of the industry and scope of growth necessary to provide for veterinarians and their teams. Findings included heavy student debt loads, lower earnings than human-medicine doctors, and a lack of business training. The American Veterinary Medical Association, the Association of American

Veterinary Medical Colleges, and the American Animal Hospital Association commissioned the study and have taken the results and used them to drive change in the industry. And yet veterinarians still list "money" as their number one source of stress.

Here's why – there are more than four times as many medical schools than veterinary schools, yet the number of people wanting to be doctors of animal medicine is nearly as high as those wanting to be doctors of human medicine. Not only is competition stiff, but the cost of veterinary school might surprise you – four-year graduate program costs range from $150,000 to nearly half a million dollars. That's on top of whatever the first four years of their college cost and most of the eight years of school tuition is carried as debt – only 19% of veterinary college students graduate with no student loans.

General practitioners of human medicine earn, on average, $180,000 upon graduation. General practitioners of veterinary medicine earn, on average, $91,000.

Now let's compare salaries – general practitioners of human medicine earn, on average, $180,000 upon graduation. General practitioners of veterinary medicine earn, on average, $91,000. That means it is twice as tough for a veterinarian to get out from under their student debt mountain as it is for a human doctor.

And as you are about to see, it's very expensive to run a veterinary hospital, so veterinarians often pay themselves last with the leftovers, after covering all the other expenses.

Ouch!

Staff Issues

This problem is like a dragon with three heads – it might be a beautiful and unusual dragon, and it's also going to be a difficult dragon to live with on a daily basis. Veterinarians go into the profession because they want to help animals. Until the KPMG study referenced above was released, veterinary colleges focused on animal care, not on skills needed to manage a staff and run a business. Animal care, staff management, and business acumen are the dragon's three heads.

Veterinary hospitals are small businesses that tend to be quite heavily staffed in relation to the revenue they generate. They have to be. While automation can streamline workflow in many industries, it's not terribly useful in hospital settings, animal or human. Veterinarians are necessary to examine and treat animals. Veterinary technicians, also known as veterinary nurses, are necessary to triage, take vitals, and assist the veterinarian in their exams and surgeries. Receptionists are necessary to manage the communication between clients, potential clients, and the hospital staff. Kennel technicians are necessary to care for animals that are hospitalized or being boarded. Groomers are necessary to provide a one-stop service when animals have been boarded or kept for treatment, and the owners want their pet to be clean, shiny, and sweet-smelling when they pick it up.

The average one-veterinarian hospital has between five and 20 additional people on staff, and if you have ever been in charge of anything, you know that people don't manage themselves. Even if the veterinarian isn't the owner of the hospital, they're the ranking staffer, so are usually the one tasked with delegating, refereeing, and soothing hurt feelings. None of this is what they went to school for or have a passion for, and most of the time, they would rather hide in their office than deal with personnel issues.

Ouch!

Business Issues

In the early years of this century, veterinary colleges began adding business courses to their curricula. While the veterinary industry is experiencing a "corporatization" of hospital ownership, well over 85% of general-practice veterinary hospitals are privately owned as of this writing. That means that it's likely that the veterinarian you and your pet see is also the owner of the practice. And because of the heavy student loan burden plus the earnings discrepancy mentioned earlier, a veterinarian is far less likely than a human doctor to add a practice manager to their staff.

Have you ever been a small business owner? Especially in the beginning years, the financial and managerial pressure can be enormous: paying for the space necessary to see patients and clients, buying or leasing equipment, hiring staff, doing enough business so you can pay the staff, figuring out how to do payroll and quarterly taxes and financial projections and billing and collections, having a website built, coming up with a marketing strategy, paying for health insurance for the staff and errors and omission insurance for the practice, understanding and following OSHA guidelines, etc. All of that requires time and attention on a daily basis. Add to that dealing with the challenges of managing human beings, dealing with difficult clients and injuries caused to staff by patients, and you have a very stressful situation for the veterinarian. And that's even before they start dealing with the medical issues for which they're trained.

Ouch!

Client Issues

If personnel issues are the three-headed dragon, then client issues are the classic double-edged sword. Yes, it is sharp and cuts well. And yes, it will cut no matter which way it's swung, and it cuts both participants in the situation if the person swinging it isn't careful.

Clients pay the bills. Clients are where the veterinary hospital gets the funds to pay the lease or mortgage each month, pay for the staff, equipment, insurance, utilities, marketing, and every other cost involved in running a veterinary hospital. Clients bring in the patients for routine and not-so-routine visits. Clients are necessary to the practice of veterinary medicine. Clients can be fabulous, so-so, or downright awful, and they have to be dealt with, because without them nothing else happens.

Sometimes clients walk in with a pet that's been critically ill for days and expect the doctor to work a last-minute miracle. Sometimes clients walk in with a sick pet and tell the vet the diagnosis they have come to, the treatment they expect and what it should cost, because they read about it on the internet. Sometimes clients walk in and expect treatment for little or no money because, "you're a vet, and you took an oath to take care of animals, so do it!" And often, in the world of social media where we now live, one irritated client can torpedo the reputation of a veterinarian or a hospital with just one post.

> As human beings, we are remarkably noncompliant when following our own doctor's orders.

Most clients are better than that, and all clients are human. As human beings, we are remarkably non-compliant when following our own doctor's orders. According to a CDC study, 20 to 30% of prescriptions for chronic medical conditions are never filled, and 50% of those people who do fill their prescriptions don't take the medications as prescribed.

If we are that bad at taking our own medications, imagine how bad we are at medicating our pets!

I recently had a dog who developed a severely ulcerated cornea. At the emergency hospital, three eye medications and one "cone of shame" were prescribed and dispensed. I got a lot of very good instructions on how to administer the meds and why the cone was necessary. Fast-forward a few days when she cried out, held that eye closed, and panted in pain. We again landed on the doorstep of the emergency hospital. The first, second, fourth, and fifth questions dealt with compliance – did I give the meds as directed, and did I keep the cone on all the time. The questions were asked in different ways several times before my dog was taken back to see the doctor. By the way, in case you were wondering, question three was whether my dog was eating and drinking normally.

Initially, I felt irritated at the implication that I couldn't follow simple instructions. Then I realized the saddest part of that line of questions – many, and maybe most, owners could not honestly say they had followed instructions.

(And thank you for worrying about her a little bit – my dog is doing well now, and she was beyond delighted to stop getting eyedrops and shed the cone when the doctor said she could.)

Imagine being the veterinarian. You spent the better part of 20 years of your life working towards becoming a hero for your patients. You graduated with staggering debt and went into practice doing a lot of things you never really wanted to do, many of which added even more financial pressure. You hang up your shingle, open the doors to your practice, and in walks The Client with The Patient. You examine, diagnose, dispense treatment, and carefully explain to The Client how to care for The Patient, so their beloved pet gets better.

And three days later, you get a call that The Patient not only isn't doing better, it's doing worse. And during triage, you learn that The Client, who loves their pet and would do almost anything for it, isn't giving the necessary medication or follow-up treatment as directed.

The person who helps ease your financial burden is the same person standing between you and their pet, preventing their pet from getting better

Now multiply that by two or three noncompliant clients per day every day you see patients.

The person who helps ease your financial burden is the same person standing between you and their pet, preventing their pet from getting better. Now imagine the kid gloves needed to get it through The Client's head that the pet isn't getting better because they're dropping the ball, not you.

Ouch.

Self-Talk Issues

Negative self-talk is the single most destructive force in a human's life. And most people have no clue the violence they are doing to themselves by not taking control of what their brain is saying to them.

The veterinary field is filled with very smart people who do very dumb things to themselves all day, every day. They do it because they don't know any better. Lots of others do it, too – maybe you? It's OK – it's a very human thing to do, for reasons you're about to learn. Negative self-talk can be unlearned, so if it is an issue for you too, this chapter can help you understand and break a very destructive habit.

I'm a professional speaker, trainer, and consultant. In order to ensure that the information and tools I give to clients are cutting-edge, I stay current in the fields of neuroscience, neuroplasticity, and positive psychology, so negative self-talk is an issue I deal with every day when working with people.

Dumb, incompetent, imposter, unpopular, and exhausted is how many veterinarians describe themselves, and, with the exception of exhausted, not one of those words could possibly be true.

Remember the personality profile of the "average" vet – introverted, perfectionist, driven, unable to easily ask for help, and unable to easily express how they feel? Remember that list of self-talk words that veterinarians admit to thinking and sometimes even saying aloud? Dumb, incompetent, imposter, unpopular, and exhausted is how many veterinarians describe themselves, and, with the exception of exhausted, not one of those words could possibly be true. How could they be, since the vet not only got into school, they graduated, passed their boards, and became a veterinarian. Dumb, incompetent, unpopular imposters can't possibly do that!

Here's a quick tutorial on how the brain works – what you say to yourself or others repeatedly becomes a belief to you. It may or may not be true, but you will believe that it is because you've trained your brain to believe it.

In the brain are synapses, and when you have a thought, two synapses near each other open up, fire tiny messenger packets at each other, the packets connect, the thought happens, and then the packets start retreating into their synapses. When most of the packets are safely back inside their own synapse, that synapse closes. A few messenger packets get stuck outside on the trail between the two synapses. The next time you have the same thought, the same two synapses open, spew packets, the packets connect, the thought happens, then the packets start retreating, and the synapses close again. And again, a few more messenger packets are stuck outside on the pathway between the two synapses.

Lather, rinse, repeat until you have had the same thought so many times that the straggler messenger packets have formed a continuous line between the two synapses. Those two synapses are connected by a bridge of messenger packets stuck between them, and what was once just a thought is now a belief. The thought is so easy to think that sometimes it feels like it's thinking you. And you don't question it, you believe it. You trained your brain to believe it by thinking that thought so often.

Athletes harness the power of this organic
brain process when visualizing a victory

Athletes harness the power of this organic brain process when visualizing a victory. It is the same process behind using affirmations to make a positive change in your life. Used constructively, this process can help you create almost any kind of positive change or outcome you want.

This process is also behind the destructiveness of negative self-talk and is why constant negative feedback given to a child will almost always produce an anxious, stressed-out adult. Sometimes even one small painful event can produce limiting beliefs. Let me give you an example from my own life.

When I was a child, I wanted to take ballet classes. Ballerinas seemed magical to my seven-year-old self, and I wanted to be magical too.

My brothers and I didn't know it, but apparently, our parents walked a financial tightrope much of the time. There just wasn't money left over after paying all the bills to indulge a little girl's impulsive dream. One night I overheard my parents talking about ballet lessons. Mom was trying to convince Dad that they could find a way to make it work. Dad was skeptical and finally said, "She doesn't need dance lessons. She's too clumsy to be taking ballet, and we'd be setting her up for failure."

Ouch. In Dad's defense, he would never have said that if he knew I was listening. I don't even think he meant it – he was just trying to find a way to save face and not have to admit that he couldn't afford something his only daughter wanted.

I didn't know any of that at the time. I just heard the man I adored and revered call me clumsy. So, since he was just about the smartest person I knew, I must be clumsy. The disappointment of not getting to take ballet lessons hurt, and whenever I thought of it, I heard the word "clumsy" again and again inside my head.

From the time I was seven until I reached my early 20's, I thought I was clumsy. I didn't like PE class – I was too clumsy for sports or gymnastics. I didn't like going to school dances – I was too clumsy to dance. I didn't say "yes" when boys asked me out – what if they discovered I was clumsy?

Meanwhile, I became quite good at horseback riding, even managing to stay on a bucking horse while riding bareback. I fell in love with dance music and even taught people how to do the Latin Hustle. As part of my radio job, I strode confidently across stages in front of thousands of people, welcoming them to concerts starring their favorite artists.

And yet I still thought of myself as clumsy, just because I overheard Dad apply the word to me once with my ears and countless times inside my own head. I created the belief in my own clumsiness. And thankfully, through using the mental stop sign exercise, I killed the belief after nearly twenty years of it controlling parts of my life.

If you suffer from negative self-talk that guts your confidence and controls your life, too, here's how to use the mental stop sign: when you think a thought that's negative about yourself, visualize a stop sign right in front of you. See the stop sign and purposefully think about something else. Do this every time you catch yourself thinking those habitual, hurtful thoughts. If you can't come up with anything else to think about, sing a song, either out loud or inside your head. You can't think and sing at the same time, so pick a song and go for it.

If you are very consistent in catching yourself in negative self-talk, the need for that stop sign will get less and less, until one day you will realize you don't believe that way anymore. The connection between the two synapses has been broken – what was once a belief is now merely a thought again. And you know how to banish it when it pops up.

Belief-creation happens slowly, subtly, and without you even knowing that it's happening. And there is another attribute about your brain that you need to know. No matter how positive you feel, your brain has a negativity bias. The very primitive part of your brain, the amygdala, gathers information from the world around you and has a 1.5 to 3 second head start over the logical, rational part of your brain, the frontal lobe. There is an evolutionary reason for this – Cave Man and Cave Woman would not have lived to produce Cave Babies without the fight-or-flight reflex that lives in the amygdala. Thousands of years later, we don't need that flood of stress hormones that controls us when we get startled, and yet there they still are.

So, take a brain with a negativity bias and also the ability to turn an idea into a belief while you are not paying attention, and voila! Negative self-talk becomes ingrained – so ingrained that the person hearing it day in, and day out, doesn't even question the validity of it. They believe they are dumb, incompetent, unpopular, and an imposter. And all of that makes them exhausted.

Ouch.

Add these stressors up – money, staff, business, clients, and negative self-talk – and on a bad day, a very good person could make a very permanent decision.

In the next chapter, you'll hear from veterinarians, in their own words, about events that have stressed them out, sometimes right up to the edge of their breaking point. And you'll understand what might cause a person to consider suicide and why there are very few suicide attempts in the veterinary field.

And in the chapters after that, I'll double-dog-dare you to take what you've learned and start saving lives.

CHAPTER 4

Suicide Stats and Stories

In Chapter 3, you learned a little bit about how brains work – the negativity bias and how synapses and messenger packets create beliefs. Constantly thinking or hearing the same thing over and over and over again creates a strong belief in it, whether it's real, true, or factual. Once the messenger packets have formed a connection between the synapses, that thought becomes a belief.

On average, veterinarians and vet techs have two conversations a week about euthanasia.

With that knowledge as your basis, here's what is arguably the biggest threat to veterinarians when the going gets tough, and they're feeling helpless or trapped: the euthanasia conversation.

On average, veterinarians and vet techs have two conversations a week about euthanasia. Clients may arrive with a pet with no chance of survival, or perhaps with an elderly pet with no outward health problems, but the owner wants to understand how and when to make the decision. The vet or vet tech explains the options, and it might sound something like this:

> "You have done the best you could for Fifi, and she's had a long and happy life. Sometimes our pets just go to sleep and don't wake up. Most of the time, it's up to us to end their pain and suffering. When she gets to that point, you'll know it – she'll tell you – and together we'll give her the best last gift possible, the end to her suffering."

If your vet says those words twice a week, that's 104 times a year. Multiply that by how many years they've been in practice, and you have an approximation of how many times their brain has fired the same messenger packets from the same synapses. And that's just the number of times they've said, "euthanasia is an end to suffering and is a gift" out loud – they've undoubtedly said it inside their head many more times. It's become a belief. And it's a benign belief when they're talking about Fifi.

It's not a benign belief when they're feeling helpless or trapped. If the stresses of their life have spiraled out of control, that belief could be the last little nudge that sends them to their controlled substance lockbox, reaching for the euthanasia solution. Or to their gun safe, if they're a gun owner.

> There are very few veterinary suicide attempts.
> They may feel like an imposter or dumb or
> unsuccessful – in fact, they're experts.

You see, veterinarians know exactly how to end a life. There are very few veterinary suicide attempts. They may feel like an imposter or dumb or unsuccessful – in fact, they're experts. And like the experts they are, when a veterinarian chooses suicide, they generally succeed.

Please set aside any cultural or religious views you may have about suicide and try to feel with your heart the pain and suffering a person has to be going through to even consider ending their own life. If you have never been in that dark, exceptionally desperate, and painful place, please understand how lucky you are and have compassion for those on a different path.

There is good news, and you could probably use some now, right? Here you go…

- Even though the suicide rate among veterinarians is high, most veterinarians will never seriously consider suicide.

- Suicide attempts are like a keyed lock – a lot of tumblers must be in exactly the right position, all at the same time, in order for the key to turn the lock.

- Ninety-five percent of those who get to the point of suicidal ideation won't act on the thoughts.

- Ninety percent of those who get to the point of suicidal desperation won't act on the thoughts or will be interrupted in the process.

- You can save a life, and you'll learn how in the next chapter.

So far, in this book, you've heard a lot about veterinarians and their stress from me. For the rest of this chapter, I want you to hear from veterinarians and vet techs as they share stories from their practices.

From Erin Stein-Jones, DVM, MPH

I am an ER veterinarian, so I have the fortune of seeing both the best and the worst of people, regardless of the time of day. Here are some of the worst.

Friday night, I had a lady with her 17-year-old terrier mix come in for overnight care and monitoring. The dog had been found unresponsive and wrapped up in a blanket earlier that afternoon. He was triaged to his regular veterinarian then sent to us for further monitoring. His regular veterinarian thought that he had had a heat stroke and/or seizure based upon his elevated temperature. When he arrived at our clinic, he was sitting up and as alert as a 17-year-old, blind, deaf terrier could be.

Shortly after the owners arrived and while they were still filling out paperwork, a young couple arrived with their cat, who had been hit by a car. The cat was somehow still alive, although in significant respiratory distress with a hemoabdomen (bleeding into the abdominal cavity) and a crushed pelvis. The female cat owner began wailing when I told her the bad news. You could hear her everywhere in the hospital that she did not want to euthanize her cat. They had limited funds, and there was very little we could have done for the cat anyway. We took care of the poor cat, and those owners left the building sobbing. They walked right past the terrier people who had been waiting for an hour (including the time walking into the clinic.)

I went up to talk with the terrier people who proceeded to tell me how disappointed they were in the wait time and how all their dog needed was to be hooked up to fluids and that they could not believe that they had been made "to wait on a euthanasia." They proceeded to question why it was taking us so long when our competitor (ER down the street) said that they had staff ready for them to walk in and be immediately hooked up to fluids. I thanked them for their patience and calmly explained that we had to complete the paperwork, present them the estimate, and review information with them as they were first-time clients, and we wanted to ensure that they did not have any questions and understood the treatments we would be doing that night. Owners calmed down slightly. I reviewed the estimate. They were fine with that until I said that the next step was to sign the consent form and leave the deposit. The female owner flipped out and stated that she could not believe that she was being made to pay for something that had not occurred yet. I stated that it is standard protocol and that we take a 50% deposit and anything else is due at time of discharge. Owner then screamed at me that she would just be going to our competitor and proceeded to storm out of the clinic and leave in her brand-new Cadillac Escalade.

The other worst story involved a foster kitten about three months of age who had never done well. Littermates were doing very well, but this kitten had always been sickly, and now she had "the sniffles" and would not eat. The foster brought her in and then informed me that the rescue did not want her there and had not approved anything. I called the rescue because they have to authorize any "non-emergent" procedures. The rescue authorized everything, and we ran bloodwork. The bloodwork was atrocious, and the poor kitten had almost no white blood cells or red blood cells. Her chemistry was not much better.

I went back in to talk with the foster. I usually review everything with them first as a courtesy because I know how much they get attached to the babies. She proceeded to interrupt me every time I reviewed something that looked poor. She then ignored everything I said and pointed out anything that was still within normal limits, and stated that the lab work looked OK and she was sure that the kitten was OK. It took about 5 minutes of her constantly interrupting me before I finally asked if she was in the medical field, to which she replied no, she was not but that she had a lot of lab work done on herself. I then stated that we needed to go ahead and call the rescue in order to review the lab work. She was so furious with me that she was visibly shaking in the room, and I still do not understand what I did that angered her so much. She berated my receptionist and kept questioning her about where I went to school. She left a nasty review calling me a joke. When she did not receive a reply to the review, she emailed our clinic and our manager separately to ask them if they had read the review and to complain about how rude I was because I kept calling her "ma'am." I live in the South.

On the good stories, I have had quite a few of these, including the owners who brought their cat in because he sounded a little bit different. Everything checked out on him. They sent a lovely thank you note to all of us.

Or the kitten that I euthanized for FIP. Not only did they send a lovely thank you note, but they addressed all of my nurses by name in the thank you note.

This week, I had a wonderful owner who happened to be a physician. His older baby had GI signs, and it was a matter of going back and forth between us and his regular veterinarian. Even though we found out later that his dog had a ruptured gallbladder and she was euthanized, he was so appreciative even when we were trying to find out what was wrong with the dog. He apologized for continuing to bother me with phone calls, which his "bothering" was only one phone call where he had additional questions. He was so respectful and kind. He didn't mind waiting over an hour for other emergencies, even though he was practically falling asleep in his chair. He just thanked us for even being there.

From Meghan Knox, DVM

I'm now doing relief work, so I'm not attached to any one hospital. It's been the best step for my mental health to basically not put roots down in any one place, so I don't get sucked into the drama, and I'm able to set my own schedule and terms! Here are a few client tales from my life as a vet that stand out:

Client called about 20 minutes before we were scheduled to close, saying she is bringing her dogs over for an emergency. We are not an ER and tried to phone triage the situation, given the time of the night. Owner wasn't hearing it and showed up about 2 minutes to close, demanding to be seen. Note we have a sign that says walk-ins welcome!

Dogs are happy and bouncing around the lobby. The practice manager forces me to see the client and thus stay late and keep staff late. One dog had a hot spot the size of a quarter, and the other dog had a few pimples, and both issues had been present for over a week.

Client was nasty and rude. I charged an emergency fee because of making us stay late. Client went through the roof. The practice manager removed the charges. As a salaried employee, I get no overtime and frequently got stuck staying late for things like this. Client was pissy that we were not wildly cheery, and I called her out that she was preventing us from going home and seeing our families for something that could have clearly been a scheduled appointment during regular business hours. Client laughed and said she didn't care, and as the customer, she is right so we could deal with it. Had to be one of the most entitled people I've ever met.

Another client had a full voicemail, so we were unable to leave a message with pre-surgical instructions for a routine preventive spay. We called multiple times and also attempted to email with no response.

Client fed the dog that morning, and so we explained that we would need to reschedule for the safety of the pet. Cue mass hysterics and screaming and client storming out. Later that morning, her father showed up to scream at us. The practice manager made me go into the room to explain the medical reasoning behind rescheduling. Man refused to listen to reason and said we were inconveniencing him (not even his dog, mind you, it belongs to his grown adult daughter) and continues screaming. Refuses to acknowledge that his daughter did not return calls to us after multiple outreach attempts.

I offered to reschedule within the next 72 hours, and he considers this unacceptable and wants the surgery done the next day when we have no availability. I explain this, and he continues to scream that it is unacceptable and then physically came towards me, screaming and swinging his arms in a rage. Then slammed the door to exam room open, screaming that he wasn't done with us yet, and we were in trouble, and stormed out screaming.

Practice manager rearranged the surgery schedule to fit him in and then took money off the bill because of us "inconveniencing" him. No support for me or any of the staff that had to deal with verbal abuse and threats and physical threats towards me. Also, loss of production due to discounts on the bill.

The customer is always right attitude makes people feel entitled to abuse other people. Hospitals should have clients, not customers, and there should be a baseline of mutual respect in that professional relationship.

I had to leave this job because this was a constant issue. Entitled clients were basically trained to scream and abuse the staff to get their way and get free stuff. No support from upper management and blindly equating client survey scores to quality medical care was demoralizing and exhausting. Who wants to go to work every day to be disrespected and feel worthless? I felt like a shell of a person, quick to defensive anger and hopelessness. My physical health suffered. My marriage suffered. My next job wasn't necessarily all rainbows, but it was better than that.

In another instance, a client brings in a dog with a lengthy history of complicated chronic diseases. Dog just not acting right, not really eating. Offer multiple diagnostics – client declines everything and says they will just take the dog home to die. Attempt to offer euthanasia if the owner feels that it is time for their pet. Client declines and wants "shot". Attempt discussion about lack of miracle shot and that given concurrent conditions just giving the dog something like a steroid could make it sicker. Discussed enticing food options and possible at-home care options. Client takes the dog home. I explain that we are open late and available in person or by phone if needed.

Client goes to another vet and allows vet to perform diagnostics and thus give client treatment options, and the dog improves with care.

Client posts on township FB page that I'm a heartless idiot that just wants to kill dogs, and the other vet cares and works miracles. Social media mob jumps on board, bashing me and the clinic. Obviously client does not explain that they declined everything, and therefore, my hands were tied.

My boss and clinic owner called the client out on the Facebook bashing and for posting false information and noted that he would forward all records to the other vet in town as they were not welcome back. Client attempted to backtrack, saying she likes the clinic just hates me. Boss stood up for me and said actions have consequences, and she cannot bash me online without bashing the entire hospital and is not welcome back. Client actually removed FB post and put up an apology for acting out emotionally due to her love for her dog. Boss still fired her. Felt good to be supported.

To balance out the bad stories, here's one about a client that just really liked me. She helps rescue cats and ends up with some complicated cases. Worked with her on diabetes management for her one cat, and the cat's overall quality of life greatly improved. She baked the clinic a lovely cake and some cookies as a sign of appreciation. Next time she was in, she asked if I had enjoyed the treats, and I had to explain that I had gestational diabetes with my pregnancy and, therefore, couldn't have any of the treats but that I greatly appreciated the thought behind such a gesture. Later that afternoon, after her appointment, she returned to the clinic with a gorgeous flower for my garden at home because she felt bad that I couldn't have the sweets. It was one of the nicest gestures a client has ever done for me. So personal and kind. Every time I see that flower in my garden, I smile and think of her even though I'm no longer working at that clinic.

From Nicholas Raimondi CVT

I was working in a 24-hour emergency practice and a 10-month-old dog presented that had been hit by a car. The dog had an open fracture and degloving wounds (the skin peeled off) to his front leg. The dog should have had surgery to repair the leg, but the owners were unable to afford the repair surgery. The veterinarian then offered amputation as an option, but the owners also could not afford this. The owners were facing the fact that they were going to have to euthanize the dog because they could not afford either surgery.

The veterinarian did not want to euthanize a young dog, so offered to treat the dog with cast and bandage changes free of charge to see if we could save the dog. We told the owner to bring the dog every other day for the first part of the treatment for bandage changes, and then once the wounds were improving, we could increase the amount of time between changes. The owners did live a bit of a distance from the emergency hospital, so we told them the decision was theirs; they could bring the dog to their regular veterinarian, or they could bring it to us, and we would do it for free.

The owners brought the dog back to the emergency clinic six months later because the leg "was really starting to stink." We looked at the dog in horror and realized that it still had the initial bandage on the leg that we put on the night of the injury. As we were taking the bandage off, the dog's leg literally fell off in the bandage. Despite what this dog had gone through, he was the sweetest boy through all of this. We all felt absolutely horrible that the dog had gone through this. The veterinarian got the owners to sign the dog over to the hospital, and the rest of the leg was amputated, and the veterinarian ended up keeping the dog herself.

From vet tech Alysha (prefers not to use her last name)

It was our last shift before Christmas 2017 and was a shortened day. We always make a post of our closures during the holidays well in advance on multiple social media platforms as well as posted on the door. I was running late after my shift, finishing my cleaning, which left me there until our typical closing time an hour after we closed that day.

I had to call my brother and was on the phone for over 40 minutes, trying to tell him he needed to take his dog to the local emergency clinic as she was not well after a dog fight and possibly eating baker's chocolate the previous night. As I am finishing up on the phone and turning out the lights, I hear a sharp tapping on the glass; a client was using her keys on the windows to get my attention as I did not hear her knocking first. At this time, I am in full winter gear with bags in hand.

I get to the door to leave, and she tries to pull it open, saying she needed to get her daughter's cat's medication. I tell her I cannot sell anything as our systems are shut down for the holidays, and I cannot send anything home without payment. She got very upset, saying she always takes the last bus to make it before we close, mind you it is now over an hour after our usual closing time. She then said, "You wait here; you're going to explain to my daughter why she can't have her cat's medication." She kept me there for about 10 minutes before I noticed my mother had just pulled into a parking space nearby, and I attempted to leave, saying I had a family emergency and needed to go. The client followed me to the car, all the while trying to get me to call her daughter.

We managed to leave without too much trouble once I was able to get into the car, but we did not make it in time to help my brother's dog – she passed away minutes before we got to his house.

From Dr. Amber Hutchinson

I am a small animal vet in Pennsylvania, and I have some pretty great clients that treat my team and me with respect, and I have always been lucky to have that. But this case, in particular, was rough...

A client called with an 11-year-old Labrador that ate 4lbs of chocolate. We are talking milk and dark mixed and enough to kill this dog multiple times over. The dog had gotten into a very small amount of chocolate earlier that year and had been fine, other than some diarrhea. So the owner thought that's all that would happen this time. The dog didn't look great, however, so the owner called us for advice. Our client service person told them that was a fatal amount of chocolate and after much bargaining and arguing, the owner reluctantly agreed to bring the dog in. This is several hours following exposure.

On presentation, my patient was happy but hyper, had a heart rate through the roof, and was dehydrated. We induced vomiting and got up about 2lbs of chocolatey fluid. Her heart rate was sky high, and I was extremely worried about a potentially fatal arrhythmia. I expressed this to the tired wife that arrived and explained that we were not an emergency clinic, so we do not have the medication or personnel required to treat this following the initial visit, but having worked as an emergency vet for a number of years, I highly recommended transferring this gorgeous lab to a 24-hour facility where she could continue treatment and be monitored and treated for potentially fatal abnormalities in her heart rate. The wife seemed to understand but wanted us to wait for her husband to arrive. I checked my patient's electrolytes and started IV fluids as well as mild sedatives to try to relax her and bring her heart rate down. We placed her in a quiet area in the dark with a technician monitoring her, and her high heart rate persisted.

When the husband finally arrived a couple of hours later, I again explained the situation. He was not convinced. Why did she have to go now when she was fine a few months ago? What guarantee do I have to give that she will die if she is not brought there, or vice versa, that she will live if she goes? Unfortunately, there are no guarantees in medicine, and all I could offer again and again was my recommendation.

The owner was irate! This was ridiculous over some chocolate! He called four other veterinary clinics and spoke with three vets and one technician who all told him the same thing. He still was not convinced. Somehow it seemed we were trying to... I'm not sure what exactly. We get no benefit from sending patients to the emergency hospital other than the health benefits of our patients.

I stayed late to assist them, explaining all of these things over and over in every way I could think of to ensure they understood how critical this could become. All the while thinking of the amazingly sweet little lab that only did what labs tend to do and found the chocolate that had been carelessly left out by an unsuspecting child.

Would my patient die tonight because I could not convince these people of the severity of this issue? How did I fail this lovely lab who wagged her tail and licked my hand and just wanted to be snuggled? What more could I do for this precious being? I became panicked that this girl would die because of me.

Eventually, the owners elected to follow my advice (and that of all of the other people they questioned) and take her to the ER. She was monitored continuously and treated for her elevated heart rate and made a full recovery.

The thing is that even though the owners eventually listened to us, I still felt like I did something wrong, even though, as an emergency vet, I had this conversation dozens of times with clients. Maybe a hundred or more.

But deep down, when people stop listening, we find fault with ourselves. Imposter syndrome kicks in, and we wonder, are we good enough? Did we do the right thing? Did we make the correct diagnosis? Is there more we could have done? It keeps us up at night; it infiltrates our personal lives and haunts our very souls. Because as many times as we have done something right, the one time something happens that is unexpected, or a client refuses to listen to our recommendations, that seed of doubt digs away at the fiber of our being and takes root, feeding on our self-doubt.

From Jeff Houser's Facebook post, in defense of Dr. Jodi Houser

An open letter to the young man who berated my wife today and trashed her veterinary practice on social media:

Your puppy died of parvovirus (parvo), a highly contagious yet preventable disease. You could have vaccinated him, but you didn't do that.

You had another dog last year that had parvo. You could have learned from that experience and vaccinated your new puppy, but you didn't do that.

Since you didn't bother to vaccinate him, I'm not surprised that you brought him to my wife's veterinary hospital with no money to treat his entirely preventable disease. You could have realized that owning a dog is a responsibility, and if you're not going to spend money on preventive care, there's a risk that you'll have to spend a lot more to treat preventable diseases. But you didn't do that. Instead, you started a GoFundMe and got other people to pay your bill for you (although not in full).

And my wife and her dedicated staff treated your puppy for days while he continued to deteriorate. They kept him clean and medicated, kept his IV fluids flowing day and night, and hoped in their hearts that he would turn a corner, but he didn't.

And so today, when things looked grim, and euthanasia seemed like the only option, my wife let you visit your puppy in her isolation room in the basement of her hospital. Since parvo is highly contagious, he couldn't be anywhere near the other animals in the hospital. Her staff gently removed him from his cage and laid him on a blanket on the floor since he was far too sick to stand. They put an absorbent pad under his rear end since parvo causes terrible diarrhea. And they let you sit with him while you considered my wife's recommendation of euthanasia.

When he had diarrhea for the umpteenth time, you could have asked her staff to change his pad. I'm sure they would have, just as they did dozens of times before. But you didn't ask.

When you noticed black garbage bags in the corner of the room, you could have asked why they were there. I'm sure her staff would have explained that every pad, blanket, IV bag, and anything else that was used in that room is considered contaminated and can't leave the isolation room while healthy animals are going in and out of the hospital. But you didn't ask about that either.

Instead, you took pictures of everything, left with your puppy (who died a little later), and on the way out yelled at my wife that her hospital was disgusting, that the isolation room smelled bad and was full of garbage. Then you went home and posted those pictures on Facebook with a grossly misleading description, implying that your dog was left to lay on the floor in his own feces, in a smelly room full of garbage down in the basement.

Your Facebook friends were immediately fired up. They started leaving Google reviews for my wife's practice even though they've never been there. They tagged the American Animal Hospital Association in your post, threatening my wife's accreditation, and suggested that you report her to the state licensing board and file a lawsuit against her.

And now you sit at home, mourning the loss of your puppy, patting yourself on the back for having "told her off" before you left today, and relishing the fact that your Facebook friends are attacking my wife online while they shower you with sympathy. You will gladly accept their sympathy, and it will never occur to them that maybe you bear some responsibility for your puppy's death. That your failure to vaccinate your puppy for a preventable disease is entirely your fault. I know it won't occur to you.

And it won't occur to you (or them) that my wife sat in her office after you left and sobbed. That she called me and asked me through tears what she should do as the first Google review appeared. That her staff felt her pain and tried to comfort her. That they all had to gather themselves and go into the next appointment as if nothing had happened. And it won't occur to you that she'll come home tonight and won't be able to leave it all at work. That she will be hurting, and that I will feel it, and her kids will feel it.

Tomorrow she will wake up, having no doubt lost sleep over all this, and go back to work to take care of her clients and their pets. And she'll do it day in and day out and from time to time absorb these kinds of shocks. She'll keep doing the things she has always done, and you can keep refusing to accept responsibility for all the things you didn't do.

Update: We are overwhelmed with all the support and encouragement we have received. I never anticipated that this post would be so widely shared. I'm happy to report that the original negative posts and reviews have been taken down. Thanks to everyone for reminding us how much kindness there is in the world.

From Susan Reece, in praise of her veterinarian

I want to comment on my vet in Ponte Vedra Beach, FL. Cary Hirsch is amazing. My dog had progressively unusual and debilitating symptoms. We were discussing euthanizing him. After extensive research, Dr. Hirsch finally diagnosed him with Addison's disease and charted a life-changing course of action. The staff was amazing through the long ordeal, and my dog lived for years after the diagnosis – he was 14 when he crossed the rainbow bridge. Long afterwards one of the staff told me that when my dog was so sick, Dr. Hirsch slept at the clinic to keep an eye on him. It still brings tears to my eyes. Beyond top-notch professionalism, Dr. Hirsch exhibits real love for his patients. I will always be grateful.

Facebook Post – Anonymous

This short essay was written by an anonymous veterinarian and posted to a support group for veterinarians. When you read it, feel it. Put yourself in the shoes of the veterinarian who stands before you, begging you to understand how she feels daily, and what she struggles with.

I am a veterinarian.

I work long hours. I work hard hours.

My hair is often pulled back. My clothes are often dirty.

I am on the floor to take my time and make my patient feel comfortable. I am standing tall and looking you in the eyes to ensure I will take the very best care of your best friend.

I am up early mornings, giving 100% of my effort to stand by my oath and do what is right in some of the most difficult decisions. I am up late nights eating dinner on the surgery table, giving 100% to come up with a treatment plan when I just want to go home and lay down.

I get praised. I get yelled at.

I know what it's like to lose your furry friend, so I open my heart and pour it out to treat you how I would want to be treated. Then I put on my best smile and rinse, wash, and repeat for the next room.

Day in and day out I see suffering animals. Day in and day out, I stand witness to the love and bond between people and their pets.

Sometimes I have to deliver good news. Sometimes I have to deliver bad news.

Sometimes I have to convince you to do diagnostics that you don't think are necessary just so I can do my job.

Sometimes you don't want to pay, and I have to use my detective skills and still try and do the best medicine.

Sometimes you give me the reins and ask me to do anything in my power to save your pet when there is nothing left for me to do but pray.

Sometimes I have to take a deep breath at the surgery table and tell myself that I am capable.

Sometimes I walk out of the clinic feeling like a hero.

I am putting my feelings aside on a daily basis to put my oath for animals first.

I am a veterinarian.

I am a community of veterinarians.

I am a community of humans doing our best for animals and their humans.

I am standing up to say not one more vet.

Be kind to your veterinarian.

We worked our whole lives to be "doctor," but before that, we were human and continue to want to be.

From Cynthia Hutt for veterinarians and their technicians after they perform a euthanasia

You've seen the end of the rainbow,
A faithful heart at rest.
If only for a moment,
You've helped the very best.

CHAPTER 5

The Rules

Even on the best of days, and even when you're on your best behavior, you can cause stress for your veterinarian. Since you have read this far, I'm hoping that you want to understand how you could be stressing them out and how not to do it ever again. That's what this chapter is all about.

There are three rules that, if every veterinary client followed, would tremendously ease the stress veterinarians feel. These rules are to respect hospital hours, treat the staff respectfully, and follow instructions.

Simple, right?

If you are like me, you are pretty particular about who treats your animals. And if you are like me, maybe sometimes you bend a rule or two. I've been lucky to have two wonderful veterinarians care for my dogs – Rebecca Kestle here in Georgia and Sandy Karn when I lived in Maryland.

Let me share a story from my own life – one where I heaped a steaming pile of stress on a vet – so you'll see how easy it can be to ruin someone's day without meaning to or even knowing you have done it.

Dr. Sandy Karn was my second vet when I lived in Maryland. I found her the day the vet I had been seeing blew it – badly. I took in a nine-day-old puppy born by C-section that the first vet had performed. The puppy shrieked in pain when touched and was lethargic and not nursing. That vet diagnosed an ear infection and sent me home with oral antibiotics. This did NOT feel right to me, and I remembered a friend who had corgis crowing about what a great diagnostician her vet was. I called her for her vet's number.

It was 12:30 on a Saturday afternoon, and I called the number my friend gave me, which was not the main hospital number. It was the number that only a few people had, and if anyone was at the hospital, my friend assured me that it was a number that got answered. Dr. Karn was there, and she said she'd wait until I got there with the puppy. Her diagnosis was very different –

a systemic infection that had gotten into the spinal fluid and possibly the brain. She prescribed a very strong injectable antibiotic that I had to purchase from the human pharmacy, along with the tiniest insulin needles that they had.

As she wrote the prescriptions, she told me to remove the puppies from their mom and bottle feed them. If the puppy had an infection at nine days of age, it was likely that the original source of the infection was the mom, who should also be seen and treated. After giving me the dosing instructions and making sure I knew how to properly give the tiny puppy a subcutaneous injection, Dr. Karn warned me that no matter what I did, it was very possible that I could lose not just this puppy but the rest of the litter. She gave me her home phone number in case I had questions, recommended a re-check in a week if the puppy survived, let me out of the hospital, and locked the door behind me so she could clean up and finally go home two hours later than she'd planned.

Let's talk about those three rules.

As you read the story, did you pick up on the fact that I violated rule #1, which is to respect hospital hours? I didn't even call until half an hour after the hospital closed and didn't arrive with the sick puppy until nearly an hour after closing time. Sure, Dr. Karn answered the phone and told me to come in. Maybe you've heard the adage, "two wrongs don't make a right?" Dr. Karn did have a choice in the matter, and yet I started that ball rolling by calling a special phone number at the hospital and basically begging to be seen outside of regular hours. That's not respectful. A better choice would have been to go to an emergency vet – they are expecting to see emergencies outside of regular veterinary hospital hours.

> Sometimes we forget that our veterinarians are not superheroes – they need to have a personal life and adequate downtime, too.

Some vets give clients special numbers, cell phone numbers, or home numbers. Do you have any of those, like my friend did? Then rule #1 applies to calling and texting your vet, too – think very carefully before you use a special number. Is the situation truly an emergency? Is it something your doctor can help with if they are not at the hospital, are not able to examine your pet and don't have your pet's records in hand? Or is your situation one that can wait until regular business hours or needs to go to the emergency vet right away?

Yes, we love our veterinarians. And sometimes we forget that our veterinarians are not superheroes – they need to have a personal life and adequate downtime, too. We need to remember and respect that.

Rule #2 is to respect all of the hospital staffers. I got lucky on this rule – Dr. Karn was the only person still at the hospital when I got there. I hope I wasn't rude to her in my frantic attempt to help a very sick puppy. Only she could truly answer that question, and she passed away in 2002 after a long and illustrious veterinary career. She cared for my dogs for 12 of the 14 years I lived in Maryland and recommended my next veterinarian, Dr. Rebecca Kestle, when I told her I was moving to Georgia. Bless you, Dr. Karn!

You read in the last chapter, in veterinarians' own words, how rudely some clients can behave. If you read the comments and stories shared on veterinary online message boards and Facebook groups, you would be astonished at just how bad it sometimes gets. Here are just a few examples:

- Clients who comment on a vet or vet tech's weight or hairstyle or makeup in a less-than-positive way.

- Clients who pitch a fit in the crowded waiting room because they don't want to be near "that vicious dog" – a dog that hasn't done anything wrong or vicious, by the way.

- Clients who show up 2 minutes before closing expecting to get a nail trim – no appointment, no call – and become belligerent when the staff tries to get them to come in the next day.

- Clients who show up with an emergency that they haven't done anything about for three days, who then get loud and obnoxious about fees when tests, fluids, medical monitoring, and hospitalization are recommended as the only things that might possibly save the pet.

- Clients who book appointments at two or three vet hospitals and take their pet to the one that fits their schedule best, never even thinking to cancel the others.

- Clients who talk to the technicians and the receptionist as if they are servants, not professionals there to help them.

- Clients who let their pets potty inside the hospital and never make a move to clean it up.

- Clients who think the rules apply to everyone but them.

Those are extremes, and the little things add up, too.

- You get a little huffy over the cost of a C-section even though you have a breed that usually has to have them.

- You get pushy about getting a multi-pet discount when this vet has only ever seen one of your pets.

- You proceed to tell the vet what you think the diagnosis and treatment should be instead of listening to their expertise.

A little respect goes a very long way towards not stressing out the people who care for your pets. Do you have eight years of training to be a veterinarian? Do you take 30 to 50 hours a year of continuing education to keep your veterinary knowledge and skills current? Do you deal with the health and ailments of animals every day?

Most of us know a lot about our pets, personally, and don't know much at all about how their little bodies work. Before you open your mouth, try to remember that your veterinarian is the expert and is the person you're paying to keep your pet(s) safe and healthy. Trust them. And if you don't trust them, then shop for a new veterinarian – don't argue with this one or try to correct them.

And by the way – take gifts to your vet and their staff now and then, not just at the holidays. It can be cookies, chocolates, you can have lunch for the staff delivered – the possibilities are endless. When organizations bring me in to talk about veterinarians and suicide with their groups, one exercise I always do is ask everyone to write a thank-you note to their veterinarian. I provide the note cards, the envelopes, and even the stamps – they just need to provide the heartfelt appreciation and put it in writing. If it's been a while since you've sent a note of thanks to your vet, now is a pretty good time to write one.

Rule #3 is to follow care instructions to the letter. Heck, many human beings don't follow their own doctors' instructions for themselves. We can be even worse when it comes to our pets.

- Do you have a pet that is tough to pill? Do you win, or do you give up?

- Do you follow an order from your vet to put your pet on crate rest, or do you just hope things will be OK if you let your pet roam loose in the house?

- Do you take your pet back in for a re-check when the vet recommends that, or do you just figure that Fifi seems to feel better, so no need to spend the time or money?

It is important to remember that veterinarians and vet techs do what they do because they want to help animals. Don't get in the way of their mission.

I am not asking you these questions to shame you — many of us have broken rule #3 at least once in our lives, myself included.

It is important to remember that veterinarians and vet techs do what they do because they want to help animals. Don't get in the way of their mission. Do everything you can to help them help your pets — we owe it to our pets and our vet.

Remember that broad brush and yet fairly accurate personality profile of veterinarians? Introverted, perfectionist, focused, loathe to ask for help, and slow to reveal their feelings? Think about these three rules from that point of view. Can you see that by following these three rules, you can make life easier and far less stressful for your veterinarian and their team?

Earlier in this chapter, I left you with a cliff-hanger – a sick puppy, a vet with a reputation as an amazing diagnostician, and a really rude new client... me. Here is the rest of that story.

I went back to Dr. Karn's hospital after the longest week of my life. As she suspected they would, they all nursed the infection from their mother; all got sick with systemic infections and all needed treatment. Here is what that week was like for me:

1. Injections of antibiotics every four hours.

2. Bottle feeding puppies every four hours.

3. Medicating an ill and distraught mamma dog who was not allowed to nurse her puppies.

4. Holding down a full-time job.

5. Sleep? That was optional, apparently.

I walked into the hospital with the whole litter in a crate. When she saw me in the waiting room, Dr. Karn smiled a semi-sad smile – it was a small cat crate that held my Siberian Husky litter. It was not my turn to be seen yet, so as the client went into her exam room, Dr. Karn peeked into my crate, saw three puppies, and asked how many puppies I started with.

Have you ever seen your vet jump for joy? I did that day – literally!

The litter born by C-section was only three puppies – a male and two females. There were three bright little fuzzy faces inside the crate. Dr. Karn's treatment protocol pulled the entire litter through, and she was ecstatic. On her way into the exam room to see the patient ahead of us, she threw up her hands and jumped high in the air.

Are you old enough to remember those Toyota commercials where people jumped for joy as the jingle singers sang, "oh, what a feeling?" If not, here's one of the commercials that was being used on TV at around the time Dr. Karn saved my litter, so you can see how she jumped that day in her hospital. Yep, it was just like this. https://www.youtube.com/watch?v=HubZ2cABBfU

When you follow these three simple rules, you may or may not actually see your vet jump for joy. What you will see is a veterinarian who is less stressed, happier to see you, and happier to listen to your input because they know you value them.

We rely on our veterinarians and their team to keep our pets healthy and in winning form. Remember not to take them for granted. Follow three simple rules and take care of the team that takes care of your pets.

CHAPTER 6

You Can Save a Life – Will You?

Did you know that you can save a life? You can.

When I read the CDC report on suicide in the veterinary field, it galvanized my heart and my business. It became clear that the people who care for pets need our care and attention, so I turned my business focus to helping veterinarians and their teams.

As part of that focus, I enrolled in a QPR Suicide Prevention Gatekeeper Training program and became a QPR Gatekeeper trainer, https://qprinstitute.com/ I teach organizations, associations, and workplace groups about how people come to believe that suicide is their only option, how to spot those people before they reach the point of no return and how to help them.

You've already learned the first part – how people might become so stressed that they contemplate ending their own life as their only solution. May I share the other two parts with you briefly? This isn't an official QPR training – this IS enough information for you to know how to help, should you ever be in the position to help someone who is in suicidal desperation.

First, know the signs. They might be subtle, or they might be very direct. Some of the things you might see or hear are:

- Giving away prized possessions

- Unwillingness to make plans, even for something they have previously enjoyed

- Avoidance – not returning calls/texts/emails, even from their best friends

- Statements like, "no one would miss me" or "no one cares anyway" or "what does it matter?"

- More direct statements like, "take my favorite guitar – I want you to have it, and I don't need it anymore" or "pretty soon you won't have to worry about me anymore" or "please watch over my sister" or "I'm just going to kill myself."

When it sounds like it might be a cry for
help, treat it like a cry for help.

It's common for us to try to rationalize what we hear as drama. We might think that Suzi's just being melodramatic, saying she's going to kill herself – she doesn't really mean it. Or we might think that Jon's just trying to get attention by giving away his guitar. Understand this – when it sounds like it might be a cry for help, treat it like a cry for help. Don't concern yourself with their motive for making the statement they made – concern yourself with letting them feel your care and desire to help them.

People who are in suicidal desperation often feel like there's no help and no way out. Show them that you are willing to help. In many cases, that's as far as the conversation needs to go – you've shown them that they matter, and their dark spiral stops, at least for the moment. You may never know for sure that you stopped a suicide, and that's got to be OK with you. Do what you can in the moment and reach out to them the next day to reinforce the fact that you care about them and what happens to them.

Suicidal thoughts often accompany depression. If you feel that the person you're with could be clinically depressed and you see or hear anything like the actions on the list above, it's time for you to get proactive.

Yes, you.

You can do this. And you may be the only one that person trusts enough to let help them, so you must do this.

It's OK – it's not hard. All you have to do is open your mouth and let your caring heart come out.

There are several good ways to ask someone if they are OK. And one really bad way. Here's what you NEVER want to say:

> "You're not thinking of doing something stupid, are you?"

For a lot of reasons, this is the completely wrong thing to say. First, it's extremely uncaring and judgmental. You are telling them that the thought process they may currently be mired in is wrong and stupid. Second, you give them no place to go in the conversation, if indeed they are contemplating suicide.

If they are, then in that moment, suicide doesn't feel wrong and stupid to them. It feels like relief or like a solution – the only solution. They're not going to argue with you if you use negative or judgmental language. They may say that they were just kidding. They may tell you that you are off your rocker and must have misunderstood what they said. They may reassure you that they're not thinking of doing something stupid, and they would be telling the truth because in that moment, suicide doesn't feel stupid to them.

They will shut down, and you won't get the chance to help them.

Here are some much better options:

- You seem really upset. Can you tell me what's going on?

- I'm worried about you and want you to feel better. Please talk to me.

- The weight of the world is on your shoulders right now. In your position, a lot of people would be struggling. Can I help you? I'm a good listener.

- In your circumstances, some people might think about ending it all. Is that how you're feeling right now? Can we talk about it?

- It feels like you're thinking about suicide. I want to help you – can we talk?

Let them talk. You listen.

After asking them to open up, shut up and listen.

Let them say whatever they are feeling without you trying to fix anything or point out where their reasoning is wrong. Let them talk. You listen. If more, non-judgmental clarifying questions are needed, ask them. And listen some more. Listen a lot. Pretend there's super glue on your lips. Listen. Even when they stop talking for a long time, keep listening. If you're sitting next to them, gently touch them. And listen.

By talking to someone about suicide, you are not "putting thoughts in their head." If you have the feeling that they are headed for or are currently in crisis, then thoughts of suicide are already in their head, and you have the opportunity and ability to avert that crisis.

How can you trust that? Let's dip into more research about how the human body perceives things. Heck, let me tell you a story that illustrates that perhaps dog bodies can do this, too!

First, the research – in 2010, a researcher at Duke University discovered that the human intestinal tract had cells resembling the synapses found in the brain. Postulating that the gut talks to the brain via the Vagus nerve and not just the bloodstream, as had been previously believed, he conducted experiments that proved his theory. Other researchers have duplicated his findings and extended what is known about how the enteric nervous system, or second brain, communicates far more than just a need for food, water, and elimination.

Have you ever walked into a room with two people in it, and even though you did not see or hear an argument, you just know you walked into one? Would you call that a gut feeling? Most people would, and now science is catching up with what we've known all along – our bodies have a way of picking up "vibes" from the air and from living beings around us.

Many years ago, I had a dog named Bonnie. She was beautiful, beautifully sound, and was a natural in the dog show ring. I took her to an outdoor show, and before she had the chance to strut her stuff for the judge, the skies opened up, flooding the ring. There was no lightning or thunder, so just like on Broadway, the show had to go on.

Bonnie hated getting her feet wet. Hated it! Even though she was one of the soundest dogs I ever owned, when we hit the wet grass, she moved like a cat with tape on her paws – every leg went in a different direction. The judge laughed at us and let us redo the down and back under the tent, where the grass was still dry. But we had to go around the ring with the rest of the dogs in our class, which meant going back out into the pouring rain and wet grass.

For some reason, an image of me as a four-year-old popped into my head. That little girl loved to play in the rain, stomping in puddles to see how far she could make the water fly. I figured, heck, I was going to get wet anyway – might as well have fun! It was that version of me, filled with glee and with a crazy grin on my face, that led Bonnie around the ring.

And to my amazement, there wasn't a protest that time. It was the one and only time in Bonnie's life that she did not protest having wet feet. And the only difference was that I was intentionally having fun that day. I can't prove it, though I do believe it – she picked up on my glee and decided to be happy, too. She felt me, just like you have felt things from other people.

So, if you're feeling like someone is in suicidal desperation, trust your gut and do what you can to save their life.

Open your mouth and let your caring heart come out.

Practice asking "the question" with a friend. Let them know what you now know about stress and suicide and the veterinary community. Share this book with them. Ask them to be part of the solution, too. And the two of you can practice with each other.

> Your role is pivotal but it is not up to you to diagnose or treat.

When you practice, you build your own confidence, so if the situation ever presents itself, it will be easier for you to help.

And here's something that might help you feel more confident and empowered – you're not diagnosing or treating the person in crisis; you're caring for them out loud and buying time for them to get professional help. Your role is pivotal – you may be the person who keeps a suicide from happening in that moment – but it is not up to you to diagnose or treat.

You are the gatekeeper – the person who opens a gate that a potentially suicidal person couldn't see. The person who shows them a path to at least a little bit of hope. And all you have to do is open your mouth and let your caring heart come out.

Keep this information on a card in your wallet, so you don't have to look it up if ever you need it. The National Suicide Prevention Lifeline https://suicidepreventionlifeline.org/ is staffed 24/7/365 with people trained to help those in active suicidal crisis.

- Phone: 800-273-8255

- Text: 741741 – text the word HOME in the US and Canada.

- Facebook Messenger crisis message page: https://www.messenger.com/t/crisistextline

If someone in your veterinarian's practice completes a suicide, please share this white paper with your veterinarian's team – this is information they will need in order to process their loss and move forward as a team. The paper is *After Suicide: A Guide for Veterinary Workplaces*, and it was researched and written through the combined efforts of the American Veterinary Medical Association, the American Foundation for Suicide Prevention, the National Association of Veterinary Technicians in America, the Veterinary Hospital Managers Association and the Veterinary Medical Association Executives.

https://www.avma.org/sites/default/files/2020-09/After-a-Suicide-A-Guide-for-Veterinary-Workplaces.pdf

Now you know. You know who veterinarians are, at the core of their being. You know the struggles they have, the stresses we inflict on them without meaning to, and the many and varied stresses they face daily.

And you know they became a veterinarian because they wanted to help animals and are called to juggle so much more in their life as a veterinarian.

Will you help them?

Will you follow those three rules every time you interact with your veterinarian?

Will you send them a thank you note now and then so they know you appreciate them?

Will you occasionally take or send a gift for the staff?

Will you let your caring heart come out of your mouth if you ever feel the need to do so?

Will you share what you now know with your pet-owning friends so they can be part of the solution, too?

Yes? You rock!

The life you save may be your veterinarian's.

A Note From Dr. Jerry Klein

Working as an emergency veterinarian in Chicago for over 30 years, I have been witness to the wonderful veterinarians who have crossed my path working alongside me in helping sick or injured pets and their owners.

Emergency medicine in itself is defined by stress: stress to the animal, stress to the owner, and yes, stress to the veterinarian in charge of caring for them both. Many times, it IS a life or death decision.

Unlike most human physicians, a lot of responsibility lays on many vets to be the best diagnostician, surgeon, gastroenterologist, dermatologist, radiologist… well, you get my point. And this to a patient that can't verbalize their problem, with much information coming second hand from their not always articulate or observant owners. Add to that the challenges of doing it all often times on a client's budget.

The hours are long, the pay, not so good in many instances, especially the young vets or owners of new clinics. The accruing debt, the isolation (often in self-contained clinics or hospitals sometimes distantly isolated), the access to medications can lead to a perfect storm that has veterinarians the dubious distinction of having the highest suicide rate of any profession in this country, a fact that many people are unaware.

I am grateful that after many years, recognition of the psychological needs and turmoil of my noble profession are being addressed.

Dr. Jerry Klein

Chief Veterinary Officer
American Kennel Club

Resources

The National Suicide Prevention Lifeline https://suicidepreventionlifeline.org/ is staffed 24/7/365 with people trained to help those in active suicidal crisis.

- Phone: 800-273-8255

- Text: 741741 – text the word HOME in the US and Canada.

- Facebook Messenger crisis message page: https://www.messenger.com/t/crisistextline

After Suicide: A Guide for Veterinary Workplaces produced by the American Veterinary Medical Association, the American Foundation for Suicide Prevention, the National Association of Veterinary Technicians in America, the Veterinary Hospital Managers Association and the Veterinary Medical Association Executives https://www.avma.org/sites/default/files/2020-09/After-a-Suicide-A-Guide-for-Veterinary-Workplaces.pdf

BluePearl Veterinary Partners - https://bluepearlvet.com/

American Kennel Club - https://www.akc.org/ https://shop.akc.org/pages/dr-jerry-klein-bio

Not One More Vet, Inc. - https://www.nomv.org/

American Pet Products pet ownership study - https://www.americanpetproducts.org/press_industrytrends.asp

American Veterinary Medical Association 2018 statistical study - https://www.avma.org/resources-tools/reports-statistics/market-research-statistics-us-veterinarians-2018

Positive Psychology article on extroversion vs. introversion - https://positivepsychology.com/introversion-extroversion-spectrum/

Centers for Disease Control study on veterinary suicide - https://www.cdc.gov/media/releases/2018/p1220-veterinarians-suicide.html

KPMG Veterinary Megastudy - https://www.avma.org/sites/default/files/resources/161-183.pdf

Toyota commercial showing how to make your veterinarian jump for joy like Sandy's did - https://www.youtube.com/watch?v=HubZ2cABBfU

QPR Institute - https://qprinstitute.com/

About the Author

Sandy Weaver is an author, speaker, trainer, mastermind facilitator, and lover of all things dog.

As the Program Director of the Center for Workplace Happiness, Sandy creates the training programs, workshops, mastermind groups, and keynotes that help people lead happier, more successful lives. As a citizen-scientist in the fields of neuroscience, neuroplasticity, and positive psychology, she weaves science and stories into interactive experiences so participants can easily lock in the learning and incorporate new ideas, tools, and behaviors into their day-to-day lives.

Sandy's been around dogs and veterinarians all her adult life. The daughter of a career military dad and a stay-at-home mom, they always had small dogs. When Sandy fell in love with wolves, her mom talked to her about the difficulty of trying to keep a wild animal as a pet and the cruelty of expecting a wild creature to behave like a domesticated one. She then took out volume 5 of the family encyclopedia and opened it to the entry for dogs. They looked at the many different breeds, and Sandy promptly fell in love with Siberian Huskies and Alaskan Malamutes because of their wolfish look.

Being a typical child, she started lobbying her parents for the dog of her dreams. Her dad said when she had a house of her own, she could have any size dog she wanted... no big dogs in their home!

So when her radio career took her to Washington, D.C., she got an apartment and her first Siberian Husky. She met people who were part of the Greater Washington Siberian Husky Club, attended a meeting or two, and her life was changed. Before attending her first one, the only thing she knew about dog shows was that old punch line, "She's so ugly I wouldn't take her to a dog show."

Now in her 40th year of Siberian Husky ownership, Sandy has not only attended dog shows; she's titled her own dogs in conformation, obedience, rally obedience, agility, pack-hiking, barn hunt, canine musical freestyle and has even had two Siberians who were excellent therapy dogs. And in 2010, she began learning how to be a conformation judge. Sandy currently judges 29 AKC-recognized breeds as well as Junior Showmanship.

And before you ask, no, she hasn't judged the Westminster Kennel Club dog show, though she hopes to someday.

To access on-demand training geared to helping you become happier and more successful, visit the Center for Workplace Happiness website:
https://www.centerforworkplacehappiness.com

To contact Sandy about training your team, reach her at: sandy@centerforworkplacehappiness.com

NOTES
Know Your Vet and Their Team

Use this page to document the people who care for your pets and for you. Remember to note those you may encounter at an emergency or specialty vet hospital. A good way to ask for a birthday is to ask what sign of the Zodiac they are, then say "that's my (or someone else you know's) sign – what day?" You'll often get enough information to send a birthday card.

	Name	Birthday/Birth Month
Veterinarians		
Vet Techs		
Receptionist(s)		

Kennel Techs		
Groomer(s)		
Hospital Manager(s)		

Contact Information

Use this page to keep your veterinary team's contact information in one place.

Hospital Name	Physical Address	Phone and Email

Hospital Name	Physical Address	Phone and Email

Notes to Help You Be Intentional in Caring for Your Vet and Their Team

Use this table to document people who made you feel cared for and/or helped your pet through a tough time as well as to track your recognition of them.

Name	What happened?	Card/gift sent

CPSIA information can be obtained
at www.ICGtesting.com
Printed in the USA
LVHW090327141122
733078LV00024B/542